Tiny Talks

A Book of Devotions for Small Children

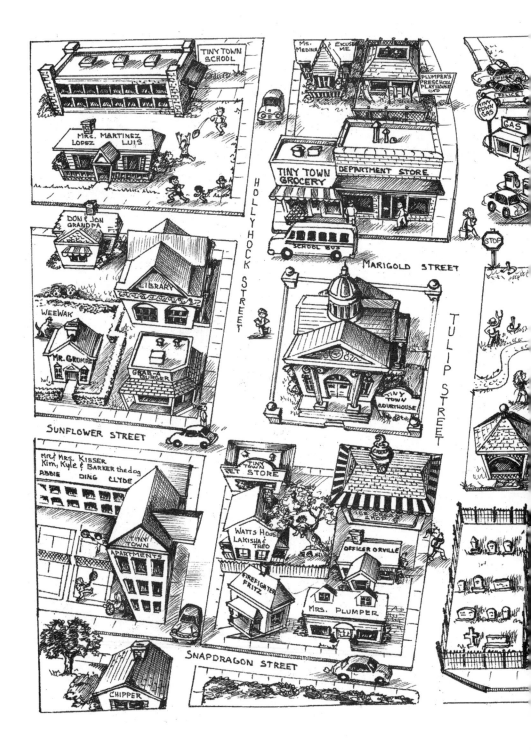

Tiny Talks

A Book of Devotions for Small Children

Robert J. Morgan

Illustrations by Ann S. Hogue

Publishers Since 1798

THOMAS NELSON PUBLISHERS
Nashville • Atlanta • London • Vancouver

To Katrina
and to
Victoria, Hannah,
and Grace

Text © 1996 by Robert J. Morgan

Illustrations © 1996 by Ann S. Hogue

Published in Nashville, Tennessee, by Thomas Nelson, Inc., Publishers, and distributed in Canada by Word Communications, Ltd., Richmond, British Columbia.

Scripture quotations are from the Contemporary English Version. Copyright © 1995, American Bible Society.

Editor: Lila Empson; Copyeditor: Dimples Kellogg; Page Designer: Harriette Bateman; Packaging: Belinda Bass; Production: Kathy Profio; Typesetting: Kathryn Murray

ISBN 0-7852-7562-2

Printed in the United States of America.

1 2 3 4 5 6 — 01 00 99 98 97 96

Introduction

How can I teach my children about God?
Why aren't my kids interested in the Bible?
Got any suggestions for family devotions?
How do I teach my children to pray?

As the pastor of a church filled with young families, I hear these questions a lot, and they deserve a good answer.

Tiny Talks is a user-friendly guide to daily devotions for families with younger children. Appropriate verses from every book of the Bible, Genesis to Revelation, are highlighted on the following pages. Each verse is illumined by a two-minute story, then punched home by a couple of interactive questions or shaped into a simple prayer you can offer with your youngster.

Along the way you will meet Lopez, a boy who tries and tries again at baseball. And Lakisha, who loves orange soda. And Theo, who hates to wear his shoes. There are also Mr. Grumps and his unsociable dog WeeWak, Grandpa and the twins, and all their friends. The residents of Tiny Town will become a family of characters your children will remember for years.

The lessons they teach will last a lifetime.

May the Lord bless your daily visits to Tiny Town— and your children's ongoing tiny (and not so tiny) talks with God.

Good Heavens

Good heavens!"

"What is wrong, Grandpa?" asked Don and Jon.

"I forgot our tent," said Grandpa. "I left it in the garage. Now we don't have any shelter tonight."

"Yippee!" shouted Don and Jon. "Now we can sleep under the stars."

The three campers spread their sleeping bags on the ground. The thick grass felt like a soft bed. They heard frogs singing and crickets chirping. The lapping of the nearby lake made them feel happy, and they looked up in the sky.

"Good heavens!" said Grandpa. "I have never seen so many stars."

"How many stars are there?" asked Jon.

"No one knows," said Grandpa. "But God made them all. He made every star you see up there, and billions and billions more. The Bible says, 'In the beginning God created the heavens and the earth.'"

"Good heavens," said Don.

"Yes," Grandpa said quietly. "The heavens are good because the One who made them is very good."

Let's talk about this:
    How many stars are there? Why do you think God made so many of them?

Respect your father and your mother.—Exodus 20:12
Read: Exodus 20:12–17

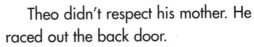

Toenails and Foot Nails

Theo hated shoes. He liked to feel mud squish between his toes. He liked for his feet to breathe.

"Put on your shoes, Theo," his mother said. "Don and Jon are coming over. We are all going to the ice-cream shop." Theo stuffed his socks under the pillow and threw his shoes under the bed.

"Are your shoes on, Theo?" called his mother.

Theo didn't respect his mother. He raced out the back door.

"Theoooooo!" his mother called.

Theo jumped high in the air and landed in a puddle. Splash! He tore across the yard and started up his climbing tree. His bare feet tightly gripped the tree trunk.

"Theo, Jon and Don are here. Are your shoes on?"

Theo jumped from the tree. A sharp pain jabbed his foot. It burned and stung. "Oww!" he cried. He fell to the ground and looked at the bottom of his foot. He had landed on an old nail. Instead of going for ice cream that afternoon, Theo had to go to the doctor.

The next time Theo's mom told him to put on his shoes, he obeyed.

Let's pray about this:
Dear God, thank you for moms and dads and aunts and uncles and grandparents and friends. Help us to always respect our parents. Help us to respect you, too.

In Jesus' name, Amen.

Do not steal. —Leviticus 19:11
Read: Leviticus 19:11–18

No-Good Candy

Angela, Abbie, and Chang were
eating candy bars in Tiny Town Park.
Angela's candy bar was chocolate.
Abbie had a caramel one, and Chang's
was peanutty. Clyde came by and
asked, "What are you no-good kids
doing?"

"Eating candy bars," said Abbie.
"We earned money for them."

"How did you earn the no-good
money?" asked Clyde.

"By helping pick up toys at the
Preschool Playhouse," said Chang.

Clyde grinned. "Look what I have,"
he said. He pulled a giant candy bar
from his pocket. It was chocolate, and
caramel, and peanutty.

"Wow!" said Angela. "Where did
you get that?"

"I stole it," said Clyde, "from Tiny
Town Grocery. They didn't see me slip it
in my no-good pocket."

Angela looked at him. "I would
rather earn a little candy bar than thteal

a big one," she said. "Thtealing ith wrong, Clyde. That ith the only no-good thing around here." Clyde slid the candy bar back in his pocket. He wasn't smiling. He looked angry. He left, and Angela, Abbie, and Chang finished their candy. They licked their fingers and threw the wrappers in the trash can.

They were glad they were earners and not stealers.

Let's talk about this:
Would you rather be an earner or a stealer? Why?

Plumper's Prayer

The children at Plumper's Preschool Playhouse had been loud and rowdy all day. Don and Jon had gotten into fights. Three-year-old Luis had run out of the bathroom in his underwear. Baby Kyle had run out of diapers. And Miss Plumper had run out of patience.

"Children," she said, "I have run out of ideas for helping you behave. Do you have any?"

"You can thend Don and Jon home," said Angela, thumb in mouth.

"You can give us all some candy," said Chang.

"We can all sit on your big lap," said Luis, pointing to Miss Plumper's lap. Miss Plumper tried not to smile, but she couldn't help it. All the children laughed. "I have a better idea," said Miss Plumper. "God is on our side, and sometimes we just need to ask him for help."

The children nodded, and Miss Plumper bowed her head. "Dear God," she said, "thank you for these children. Help us to have a good day. Help me to be happy and strong. In Jesus' name, Amen."

"Do you feel better now?" asked Don.

"I should say so," said Miss Plumper. "I should say so."

Let's pray about this:
> Dear God, thank you for being on our side. Thank you for helping us. Help me obey you today.
>
> In Jesus' name, Amen.

We have a God who is close to us and answers our prayers. —Deuteronomy 4:8
Read: Deuteronomy 6:4–9

Who Is God?

Chipper was babysitting Lopez and Luis while their mother was away. Lopez and Luis were glad, for Chipper played ball with them. He read stories to them and told them about his girlfriend. Now it was bedtime. Luis was already asleep, but Lopez wasn't sleepy at all. He was lying in bed thinking.

"Chipper," he asked, "who is God?"

Chipper said, "Well, hey, God is the person who made the stars and clouds and trees. He made dogs and cats and birds and bugs. He even made you and me."

"What is he like?" asked Lopez.

Chipper thought about that question. Then he said, "He loves us and listens when we pray."

"What does it mean to pray?" asked Lopez.

"Well, hey," said Chipper, "I can show you better than I can tell you." He bowed his head and closed his eyes. He said, "Dear God, thank you for making Lopez and Luis and me. Thank you for loving us. Please help Lopez to get real sleepy real fast. In Jesus' name, Amen."

Chipper opened his eyes. And pretty soon Lopez closed his.

Let's talk about this:
Why did Chipper close his eyes? Why did Lopez close his?

A Swing and a Miss

I will never hit the ball," said Lopez. Chipper had thrown him the softball ten times in a row, and he had swung at it ten times. He had missed every time. He felt like crying but decided not to, for he didn't want Chipper to know he cried. But Lopez couldn't hide his long, sad face.

Chipper suddenly threw the softball over his head and caught it. He threw it behind his back and caught it. He threw it with one hand and caught it with another. Then he pulled two more softballs out of his gym bag. He started juggling them. He had all three balls spinning through the air, and he caught them every time.

Lopez grinned. Chipper looked funny with his brown hair stuffed under his baseball cap. He stood on one leg, juggling three balls, and making funny faces. Lopez laughed and asked, "Where did you learn to do that?"

"Well, hey," said Chipper, letting the balls fall to the ground. "It took me a long time. I had to practice. Hitting the ball takes a lot of practice, too. The Bible says, 'Don't be discouraged.'"

Lopez picked up his bat, and Chipper threw him another ball. Lopez missed again—but he didn't stop trying.

Let's pray about this:
Dear God, thank you for helping us learn things. Help us to work hard at whatever we do.

In Jesus' name, Amen.

We praise you, LORD! —Judges 5:2
Read: Judges 5:1–3

Listen to the Mockingbird

Firefighter Fritz sat under the tree listening to a mockingbird. Lopez came along and sat on the grass beside him. "Well, hello, son," said Firefighter Fritz. "You look like a happy boy today."

Lopez put his arms around his knees and looked up at his friend. "I hit a home run," he said. "We were playing baseball, and I finally hit the ball. I hit it so hard that Chipper had to run after it. And I ran all around the bases."

"Well," said Firefighter Fritz with a smile, "that explains it."

"Explains what?" asked Lopez.

"Why this mockingbird has been singing so much! She must have seen you hit your home run, and she is happy about it."

Lopez laughed. "That mockingbird always sings," he said.

Firefighter Fritz chuckled. "Yep, I guess you are right. Birds just sing all the time. I guess it's their way of praising God."

"Praising God?" asked Lopez.

"Yep," said Firefighter Fritz, "God is so good that the birds just sing about it all day long." Lopez thought that was an even better thing to sing about than his home run.

Let's talk about this:
    Why do the birds sing to the Lord? Why should we sing to the Lord, too?

Blessings

The large pepperoni pizza sat in the middle of the table, sliced into ten big pieces. Theo and Lakisha were starved, but they bowed their heads. Mr. Watts prayed, "Dear Lord, thank you for this large pepperoni pizza with extra cheese. Bless us as we eat it. In Jesus' name, Amen."

Theo and Lakisha battled for the first piece. Lakisha won, but Theo ended up getting the last piece.

"Dad," said Lakisha as she swallowed her final bite.

"Yes, Lakisha," said Mr. Watts.

"Why do you ask God to bless us?"

Mr. Watts leaned back and said, "Well, Lakisha, it's this way. God is very good, and he gives us good things. He gives us air to breathe. He gives us food to eat and clothes to wear. He helps us be happy. When we ask him to bless us, we are just asking him to keep giving us all we need. Just like tonight. He blessed us with this pizza."

Lakisha thought about it a moment, then asked, "Do you think he might bless us with a banana split, too?"

Mr. Watts laughed. "I think he just might," he said.

Let's pray about this:
Dear God, thank you for giving us everything we need. Please continue to bless us.

In Jesus' name, Amen.

Praying Without Talking

What is wrong, Grandpa?" asked Don and Jon.

"I think I'm losing my mind," said Grandpa. "I can't remember where I left my fishing pole. I thought you boys might want to go fishing today."

"Guess what we want to do, Grandpa," said Don.

"Go fishing, like I said!" said Grandpa.

"Not today," said Jon.

"Want to play with Lopez and Theo?"

"Not today," said Jon.

"How can I know what you want to do?" asked Grandpa. "I can't read your minds. Only God can read thoughts." The twins looked at each other.

"You mean God knows what our brains are thinking?" they asked.

"Of course," said Grandpa. "That is

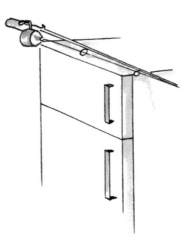

why we sometimes pray without even talking aloud. We can pray in our minds, and God hears us. Now, what do you boys want to do today?"

"Go swimming!" said Don. "And by the way, you left your fishing pole on top of the refrigerator."

"Good heavens!" said Grandpa.

Let's talk about this:
> Who can read our minds? Do you ever pray without talking out loud?

I Drank Your Drink

The sun stood in the middle of the sky and the day was hot. Plumper's Preschoolers were eating ham sandwiches with pretzels and orange sodas in Tiny Town Park. Luis drank his soda too soon. He gulped it all down before he finished his sandwich. The bread and ham and pretzels were stuck in his mouth, and he needed to wash them down.

He tried to tell Miss Plumper, but his mouth was too full. "Ahhh neeed domding ta dwaaank," he said. A half-eaten pretzel oozed from his mouth like mush. Miss Plumper just said, "I should say so!" and smiled. Luis ran over to Abbie, grabbed her soda, and raised it to his mouth. Abbie screamed at him, but she didn't reach him fast enough. In five big swallows, Luis had drunk every drop.

Miss Plumper pulled Luis to one side. She looked unhappy, and soon Luis looked unhappy, too. After they finished talking, Luis felt bad. He walked over to

Abbie. He said, "I'm sorry I drank your drink."

Abbie was sorry, too, but she forgave him. He smiled, and some more pretzel gunk oozed from his mouth. "Come on, Luis," Abbie said, "I'll give you a ride to the water fountain."

Let's pray about this:
Dear God, thank you for forgiving us when we disobey you. Help us to always say "I'm sorry" when we need to.

In Jesus' name, Amen.

Obey the LORD our God and follow his commands with all your heart. —1 Kings 8:61
Read: 1 Kings 8:54–61

Laws for Lakisha

Ten-year-old Lakisha stopped at Tiny Town Grocery for an orange soda, then started across the street. She heard a whistle. It was so loud and sudden and piercing that Lakisha dropped her soda. "Lakisha Watts, you are jaywalking," Officer Orville shouted. Lakisha didn't know what jaywalking was, but Officer Orville told her. "You crossed the street at the wrong place," he said. "You should only cross at the corner near the stop sign. It's the law."

Lakisha just stood there, feeling scared. Finally she asked, "Are you going to put me in jail?"

Officer Orville smiled. "No. But you should obey the laws. Laws are there to protect us. You might have been hit by a car."

Lakisha nodded. She thought of something her dad had told her the night before. Mr. Watts had said that God has given them a book called the Bible with rules for them to follow.

Lakisha said, "My dad said the same thing about God's laws."

"Your dad was right," said Officer Orville. "You need to obey my laws and God's laws, too." Lakisha nodded. A few minutes later she even smiled, for Officer Orville bought giant-sized orange sodas for them both.

Let's talk about this:
What book tells us about God's laws? Why should we obey them?

First Sunday

Kim Kisser didn't want to go to church. She had just moved to Tiny Town with her parents and baby brother. She didn't know anyone yet, and she didn't have any friends. She felt frightened, going to a new church. She wanted to stay home.

"We shouldn't stay home," said Mr. Kisser, sitting on Kim's bedside.

"Why not?" asked Kim.

"Because the Bible tells us to worship God."

"Can't we worship God at home?" asked Kim.

"Well, yes," said Mr. Kisser. "We are to love God all the time. We should always pray to him and sing about him. But the Bible tells us to worship God with other people, too. Everyone needs to worship in church."

"But I don't know anyone there," said Kim, fighting her tears.

"I don't either," said Mr. Kisser. "But don't you think God will help us make friends if we worship him? If we sing and pray and obey him?"

Kim nodded. And a little later, Kim Kisser went to Tiny Town Church for the first time—but not for the last.

Lakisha and Lopez and Don and Jon saw to that.

Let's pray about this:
Dear God, thank you for our church. Help us to worship you every day and every Sunday.
In Jesus' name, Amen.

Miss Plumper's Favorite Book

Angela was sitting by herself, sucking her thumb, when Miss Plumper sat on the floor beside her. "What are you doing?" asked Miss Plumper.

Angela, thumb in mouth, said, "Juth thitting here thucking m'thumb." Angela loved sucking her thumb, but she could never make her *s* sounds with her thumb in her mouth. "It ith a little thore," she said.

"Maybe it's sore because you suck it all the time," said Miss Plumper.

"Don't be thilly," said Angela. "I thuck it because it tidth me over between mealth." She gave her thumb another good suck or two, then asked, "You going to read uth a Bible thtory today?"

"I should say so!" said Miss Plumper. "I read a Bible story every day in Plumper's Preschool Playhouse."

"Good," said Angela, nodding her head up and down. "I like Bible thtorieth. I like every thingle one."

Miss Plumper laughed. "Well, I'm glad, Angela. Because everything in the Bible is true. The Bible is God's special book. It's full of wonderful stories and promises and rules. It's my favorite book."

Angela nodded, thumb still in mouth, and said, "I thould thay tho!"

Let's talk about this:
What book does Miss Plumper read every day? Why?

King Phatts

It was Bible story time. The children gathered around Miss Plumper, and she said, "Once upon a time there was a king with a funny name—Jehoshaphat. Phatts for short. One day Phatts walked atop his palace and saw armies and armies coming toward him. They weren't nice and they weren't clean. They were mad and they were mean. Would you be scared if bad people came toward Tiny Town? I should think so!

"But Phatts didn't fear and Phatts didn't faint. He said, 'Just give me time to think.' So he thought and he thought and he prayed and he prayed. Then he said to his people, 'Don't be afraid.' He said, 'They come to us with spear and sword, but they don't know we have the Lord.' So the people sang and the people prayed, and almighty God came to their aid."

Miss Plumper continued, "Know what happened? When Phatts and his people prayed, God confused their enemies. The bad men ended up fighting each other. And the city was saved.

"Now, boys and girls, do you think Jehoshaphat praised the Lord that day?"

And all the children said, "I should think so!"

Let's pray about this:
Dear God, thank you for watching over us all the time. Keep us safe both day and night.

In Jesus' name, Amen.

Better Than TV

Why did you turn off the television?"
wailed Don and Jon. "Our favorite show
is coming on."

"We have watched enough television," said Chipper. "We don't want
your Grandpa to know we have
watched TV all night, do we? Television
wastes our time."

"But, Chipper," said Don, "Grandpa
won't mind."

"Well, hey, I mind," said Chipper.
"Too much TV hurts your eyes. Too much
TV hurts your brain. And—" The twins
waited to see what Chipper would say
next. "And too much TV leaves too little
time for tickling." Chipper jumped on
top of the boys and started tickling them.
They laughed and laughed. Then they
rolled on top of Chipper and tickled him
until tears came to his eyes. Later when
Chipper was tucking them in, he said,
"Too much TV takes time from more
important things—like reading the
Bible."

Chipper started reading some Bible verses to Don and Jon. He read about Ezra who studied and obeyed the Bible all his life. The boys fell asleep that night feeling very safe and happy. Chipper smiled. He knew something very important. He knew that Bible verses are better than TV shows.

Let's talk about this:
What is more important than TV shows? Why?

Whining or Shining

Lopez rolled out of bed and looked outside. It was pouring. Big puddles had formed in the yard. He padded to the kitchen.

"Chipper was going to take me swimming today," he said, feeling sorry for himself. Mrs. Martinez sat a plate of pancakes on the table. Lopez wasn't hungry. She gave him his orange juice, but he didn't feel thirsty. "I'm bored," he said. "Maybe we can go swimming anyway."

"In this rain?" said Mrs. Martinez.

"Well," said Lopez, "we are just going to get wet anyhow. I'm going to hate being in this stupid house all day."

Mrs. Martinez sat down beside Lopez. "Son, God wants you to be happy and strong," she said. "Every day you have to decide if you are going to shine or if you are going to whine. Be thankful for today! You can read and play with your toys and organize your baseball cards. You can draw and color and help with housework. I might even let you put on your swimsuit and play in the mud if the rain slacks off. But only if you are a shiner and not a whiner." Lopez smiled and reached for his fork. He decided that he would shine—even if the sun didn't.

Let's pray about this:
Dear God, thank you for rainy days and for sunny ones. Help us be shiners and not whiners.
In Jesus' name, Amen.

Cold Feet

Theo looked in the bed and under the dresser. He looked from one end of his room to the other. He looked in Lakisha's room. He looked in the bathroom and closets. He looked high and low.

His shoes were gone.

"You can't find your shoes," said his mother, "because this house is a mess. It's so cluttered and scattered that we can't find anything. We need to clean it up."

Theo didn't like to clean house. "But God wants us to be helpers," his mother said. So Theo picked up his toys, and rested. Then he picked up his clothes, and rested. Then he straightened his bed covers, and rested. Then he helped in the kitchen. Soon the whole house was clean.

But Theo's shoes were still missing.

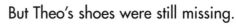

"Let's think," said Mrs. Watts, putting her finger on her nose. "What were you doing when you took them off?" Theo thought about it. He remembered his feet being very hot. He thought some more. He remembered wishing his feet were cool. He thought some more. Then he remembered. He found his shoes right where he had left them—on the third shelf . . . behind the cheese . . . in the refrigerator.

Let's talk about this:
> Why didn't Theo like cleaning up the house? Why did he help his mother anyway?

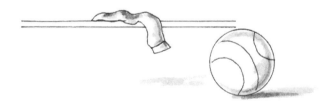

[God] suspended the earth on empty space. —Job 26:7
Read: Job 26:6–14

A World to Enjoy

Abbie rolled her wheelchair to the flower garden. The rosebushes, she thought, needed someone to admire them.

"Oh, how beautiful you are!" she said aloud, looking at a red rose. It was as big as an apple and as bright as Tiny Town's fire truck. "And you, too!" she cried, seeing a white rose.

Abbie watched a bumblebee buzzing through the bushes. She saw a family of ladybugs that had settled among the pink roses. "What a happy home you have," she told them.

Then she lifted her face and noticed the clouds in the sky. They looked like giant rosebuds, too, and the sun was turning them red. "What a beautiful world you have made, dear God," Abbie said aloud. "Thanks a bunch for roses and clouds and ladybugs—even for bumblebees."

Abbie had all God's world to enjoy.

Let's pray about this:
Dear God, thank you for flowers and gardens and clouds and bugs. Help us always enjoy your beautiful world.

In Jesus' name, Amen.

Growling Grace

Kim Kisser wanted to show her dog to
Don and Jon. She put a leash on Barker
and started off. Her mother helped her
across the street, but after that she was
on her own. Suddenly she saw a strange
boy coming toward her. He was older
than she was, and he didn't look kind.
Barker growled a little.

"What is your no-good name?"
asked the boy.

"Kim," said Kim. "Kim Kisser. What
is yours?"

"Clyde," said Clyde. "You new
around here?"

"Yes," said Kim. "We just moved
here last week."

"Where do you live?" Kim didn't
want to answer. Clyde said, "I asked
you a no-good question." He came closer, and for a moment Kim felt afraid.
Then Barker growled. "Does that no-
good dog bite?" Clyde asked.

"Maybe he does," said Kim. Barker
growled again, a little louder.

Clyde left. Later Kim told her mother what had happened. Mrs. Kisser smiled. "I was watching you from the window," she said. "And God was watching over you, too."

Kim smiled. "I guess that is why I wasn't afraid," she said. "Between God and you and me and Barker, that bully didn't have a chance."

Let's talk about this:
Who was watching over Kim? Who else?

The Hotshot's Slingshot

It was Bible story time. The children gathered around Miss Plumper, and she said, "Have you heard of David? He was a boy in the Bible with a heap of sheep. A heap of leaping, peeping sheep. Black sheep. White sheep. Dark sheep. Light sheep. And several shades of gray. They were crabby, flabby, shabby sheep. But they were David's sheep. They were his flocks. They were his friends.

"Well, one day in the grassy ground a lion and a bear prowled around. They snarled and they growled. They roared and they howled.

"They wanted some lunch! And they had a hunch they could crunch and munch on a shoddy bunch of crabby, flabby, shabby sheep.

"But David was there with his sling and his rocks. He was watching over his helpless flocks. He whirled the stones around and around, and let them go without a sound. They flew through the sky as pretty as punch . . .

". . . and the lion and the bear missed their lunch."

Miss Plumper continued, "Boys and girls, God loves us like David loved his flocks. He cares for us like David cared for his sheep. He is our Shepherd. Aren't you glad?"

And all the boys and girls said, "I should say so!"

Let's pray about this:
Dear God, thank you for being our Shepherd. Keep us in your care today.
In Jesus' name, Amen.

Beauty fades away, but a woman who honors the LORD deserves to be praised. —Proverbs 31:30
Read: Proverbs 31:10, 28–31

God's Makeup

Kim looked in the mirror. She had pretty eyes and a pleasant face. But that freckle on her upper lip! She hated it. She lathered a washcloth with soap and scrubbed. But the freckle would not budge. She put toothpaste on the end of her finger and rubbed it into her lip. She found her mother's makeup. She tried creams and lotions and powders. She was sure vanishing cream would work, but it didn't. The freckle would not go away.

Suddenly her mother came into the bathroom. "What are you doing in my makeup?" she asked.

"Trying to get rid of this awful freckle!" Kim said, bursting into tears.

When Mrs. Kisser spoke again, her voice was softer. "I kind of like your freckle," she said. "But looking good isn't about freckles anyway."

"It isn't?"

"Of course not," said her mom.

"When we love God, he helps us be happy. And when we smile and look cheerful and pleasant, our faces are lovely. And that kind of beauty never fades."

Kim thought a minute and smiled at her mother. "I guess that is why you are so pretty, huh?" Mrs. Kisser just smiled.

Let's talk about this:
Why was Kim unhappy? What kind of person is really good looking?

Mr. Grumps

"**W**hy is Mr. Grumps so grumpy?" asked Don. "He stays in his house all the time and keeps the shades down."

"Well, I have an idea about it," said Grandpa. "I might tell you if you will help me weed these hollyhocks." Don flopped on the grass and started pulling weeds out of the flowers. He said, "Grandpa, when he leaves his house, he slams the door. He never smiles. Even his dog WeeWak is grumpy. He growls at me through the hedge."

"Well," said Grandpa, wiping the sweat from his forehead. "I think Mr. Grumps decided to be grumpy when he was your age. I don't think he prayed or sang or went to church or loved God. I don't think he kept his Creator in mind while he was young."

"But that was a long time ago," said Don.

"It was," said Grandpa, nodding his head. "But if you don't enjoy God when you are young, you probably won't enjoy life when you are old."

Just then they heard WeeWak growling through the hedge. "Grandpa," said Don, pulling another weed from the hollyhocks. "I think WeeWak made up his mind to be grumpy early in life, too."

Let's pray about this:

Dear God, thank you for being our Creator, for making us. Help us to remember you while we are young.

In Jesus' name, Amen.

The very mention of your name is like spreading perfume. —Song of Songs 1:3
Read: Song of Songs 1:1–4

In Jesus' Name

Lakisha licked her ten fingers. They were covered with sticky, icky, gooey, gummy marshmallow.

"Nothing is better than marshmallows over the campfire," she said.

"Me, too," said Theo. "I like them, too. I want another one."

Mr. Watts laughed. "They are all gone, Theo," he said. "It's bedtime. You need to jump in your sleeping bag and say your bedtime prayers."

That reminded Lakisha of a question she had been thinking. "Why do we always say 'in Jesus' name' when we pray?" she asked.

"Well," said Mr. Watts, "it's like this. Jesus is God's Son. Jesus is also our Friend. And Jesus tells us that we can pray to his Father in his name. When we pray in Jesus' name, God hears us just like he hears Jesus. God listens to us just like he listens to his Son."

"I like the name Jesus," said Lakisha. "I like it very much."

"So do I," said her dad. While he put out the campfire, Lakisha washed her hands. She put on her pajamas and crawled into her sleeping bag. Just before falling asleep she said her prayers . . .

. . . in Jesus' name.

Let's talk about this:
Who is God's Son? Does he want us to pray in his name?

Don't be afraid. I am with you. —Isaiah 41:10
Read: Isaiah 41:10–13

Always Everywhere

Kim Kisser licked her huckleberry ice cream and looked at Firefighter Fritz. He was gobbling down a double cone of double fudge. Some of his ice cream had dripped on his uniform. Firefighter Fritz always wore a blue uniform, and it usually looked a little rumpled. Kim smiled.

"Have you always been a firefighter?" she asked.

"Yep," he said, his mouth full of ice cream. "My daddy was a firefighter in Germany. So when I grew up, I became a firefighter, too."

"Is it scary?" asked Kim.

"Sometimes," he said. "But I just remember that God is near me all the time. I don't have to be afraid."

"Can God be everywhere at once?" asked Kim.

Firefighter Fritz stuffed the rest of the cone in his mouth. He chewed it once, swallowed, and wiped his chin. "Yep," he said. "God can be in Germany and in America at the same time. In fact, he fills heaven and earth. He is everywhere."

"Wow!" said Kim. "That means we can never be anywhere God isn't."

"Yep," said Firefighter Fritz. "We can never be anywhere God isn't."

Let's pray about this:
Dear God, thank you for always being everywhere. Help us remember that you are always near.

In Jesus' name, Amen.

Excuse Me

I love the first grade," said Kim Kisser, opening a can of orange soda. "I love my teacher, Ms. Medina. She has a parrot in the classroom."

"A parrot?" said her dad. "In the classroom? What is its name?"

"Excuse Me," said Kim, taking a big swallow of her soda.

"What is its name?" Mr. Kisser said a little louder.

"Excuse Me," said Kim.

"Can't you hear me?" said her dad even more loudly. "I said, 'What is the parrot's name?'"

"Excuse Me," said Kim. "That is its name. That is what it says all day." Kim made her voice like the parrot's. "Squawk! Excuse me! Excuse me!"

Her dad laughed. "Well, those are good words to know. Whenever we do something rude or unkind, we need to say `excuse me.'"

"Why?" asked Kim, taking another big swallow of her drink.

"When we say `excuse me,' it means 'I'm sorry I was rude.'"

Just then Kim burped. It was a very loud, very long burp. Her dad looked over at her. "What did you say the parrot's name was?" he asked.

Kim grinned. "Excuse Me," she said.

Let's talk about this:
   What kind of bird did Ms. Medina have? What should we say after we do something rude?

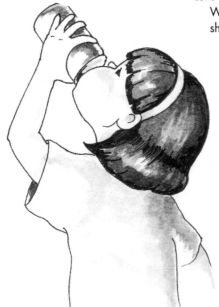

The LORD's kindness never fails! —Lamentations 3:22
Read: Lamentations 3:19–24

Power Pal

Chipper?" asked Luis. Chipper was babysitting Luis and Chang one night while their mothers and Lopez attended a meeting.

"Chipper, can you fix my Power Pal? The leg is broken off."

"Well, hey, I will try," said Chipper. He took the doll and tried to fix the leg. He pushed and pulled, twisted and turned. But it would not fit back on.

"Sorry, bud," said Chipper. "Can't do it."

Luis looked as though he would cry. "Why can't you fix it?" he asked.

"Well, hey," said Chipper. "I tried my best, but I failed."

"What does it mean to fail?" asked Chang.

"It means we just can't do some things," said Chipper. "We try our best, but sometimes we flop. Crash. Fizzle. Strike out. Get clobbered."

"Does everyone fail?" asked Chang.

"Everyone sometimes fails at some things," said Chipper. "Everyone but God. He loves us and his love never fails. He loves us all the time, no matter who we are or what we do."

Chang nodded his head. "Even when we flop, crash, fizzle, strike out, get clobbered," he said.

Let's pray about this:
Dear God, we know that you can never fail us. Help us to trust you each day.

In Jesus' name, Amen.

I will . . . give you . . . a desire to be faithful. —Ezekiel 36:26
Read: Ezekiel 36:25–28

Sunday Morning

It was Sunday morning, and Don and Jon looked out their window. The sun had already starting climbing in the sky, and it was going to be a beautiful day. They were excited. They were going somewhere special.

Were they going to the lake?

No.

Were they going to the pet store?

No.

Were they going to Plumper's Preschool Playhouse?

Not today.

Were they going to the playground?

Not now.

Were they going to the ice-cream shop?

Nope.

They were going to meet with their other friends who loved Jesus. They were going to study their Bibles in Sunday school. They were going to sing and pray and praise the Lord. They were going to learn about Jesus. They were going to church. They bathed and put on clean underwear. They dressed in nice clothes and combed their hair. They were glad it was Sunday.

Let's talk about this:
  Where were Don and Jon going? What were they going to do at church?

God made the four young men smart and wise. They read a lot of books and became well educated. —Daniel 1:17
Read: Daniel 1:8–17

School Daze

Theo was sitting in his climbing tree, feeling worried.

"How about an orange soda?" said his dad, looking up at him. Theo nodded. Soon they were sitting on the patio with their drinks. Theo said, "I don't want to go to school. I don't think I will like Ms. Medina."

Mr. Watts smiled. "Kim Kisser loves the first grade," he said. "She said Ms. Medina even has a parrot named Pardon Me."

"Excuse Me," said Theo.
"Did you burp?" asked his dad.

"The parrot's name is Excuse Me," said Theo. "And I'm not going to school next year."

"Theo," said Mr. Watts, "God has given you a good mind. Your brain can think and study and learn. God wants you to read books and solve problems and know things. School is fun because learning is fun. You will love books. Reading is fun! And best of all, you can read the Bible for yourself. Yes, I think you will like Ms. Medina and her parrot."

Just then Theo burped. "Pardon me," he said.

"Do you mean 'Excuse Me'?" said his dad, smiling.

Let's pray about this:
Dear God, thank you for our brains. Teach us to read good books and to think wise thoughts.
In Jesus' name, Amen.

If you obey me, we will walk together. —Hosea 14:9
Read: Hosea 14:4–9

Poor Clyde

Ping! Whish! The stone flew from the slingshot and hit a robin. Clyde ran over to the bird and grinned. It was dead. Just then Angela, Chang, and Abbie came along.

"What are you no-good kids doing?" asked Clyde. Abbie saw the bird lying on the ground.

"Oh, the poor robin," she said. "What happened?"

"I shot it with my no-good slingshot," said Clyde.

Angela put her thumb in her mouth and felt like crying. Abbie looked at Clyde and said, "God made the birds, and he wants us to take care of what he has made. When we obey him, we are his friends. When we disobey him, we are acting like his enemies."

"How do I know what God wants me to do?" said Clyde.

"The Bible says that God loves the birds of the air," said Chang. "I think we should take care of what he loves."

"Well, I don't," said Clyde, walking away.

"I hate Clyde's thlingthot," said Angela.

"Poor Clyde," said Abbie.

Let's talk about this:
   What did Clyde do? Why did Abbie say, "Poor Clyde"?

Rain

Abbie, Angela, and Chang looked at the sky. The clouds were dark, and Angela stuck her thumb in her mouth. "It lookth like a thtorm," she said.

Chang said, "We had better hurry." He started running through the park. Abbie was pushing as fast as she could. They rushed around the corner and saw Clyde, aiming his slingshot at a bird. The wheel of Abbie's wheelchair ran over his toe. Clyde dropped his slingshot and started hopping on one foot.

"Oww!" he shouted. "That was my no-good toe!"

The kids shouted "Sorry!" but they didn't stop. They raced back to their apartment building just in time. It poured cats and dogs. Chipper walked by.

"Quite a storm, isn't it?" he said. The kids nodded. They seemed sad.

"Well, hey! God sends the rain," he said. "It helps the grass grow and the flowers bloom. It helps the plants that give us food. It makes the rivers and lakes full, so we can swim and fish. And sometimes we can even see a rainbow if we look hard enough."

"Best of all," said Chang, "sometimes it makes us run over Clyde's no-good toe."

Let's pray about this:
Dear God, thank you for sending the rain. Help us to worship you on sunny days and on rainy days, too.

In Jesus' name, Amen.

Good or Evil

You had better not play with Grandpa's favorite fishing pole," said Don.

"I will put it right back," said Jon. "I'm going to play a trick on WeeWak."

Don grinned. "I will help you," he said. The two boys pushed the long pole through the hedge. They could see through the leaves. WeeWak was curled up in a little fat ball, sleeping. They gave WeeWak a hard poke, and the dog yelped. He jumped up, turned, and grabbed the fishing pole in his mouth. It broke during the struggle. Don and Jon were scared. They hid what was left of Grandpa's favorite fishing pole.

Later Grandpa asked, "Have you boys seen my fishing pole? I have lost it again."

"No," said Jon and Don. They both lied, but they felt very bad. They had chosen evil instead of good. They lied because they were afraid they would be punished. But they felt so bad, they finally told the truth.

"Well, I'm going to have to punish you boys," he said. "No more fishing or swimming for a week."

He looked angry. But he was also proud. He was proud that Don and Jon had been honest and had told him what they had done.

Let's talk about this:
Why was Grandpa angry with Don and Jon?
Why was he proud of them?

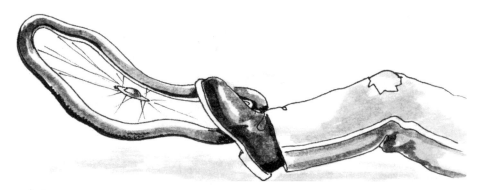

Crash!

Mr. Grumps looked over at Don and Jon. He didn't smile. He didn't say, "Hello!" He didn't nod his head. He just jumped in his car and slammed the door. He backed from his driveway without seeing Officer Orville. Crash! Mr. Grumps's car hit Officer Orville's bicycle, and the police officer wrecked.

Mr. Grumps jumped out of his car and ran over to help. Officer Orville's pants were torn and his shirt was dirty. He wasn't happy. He pulled out his book and wrote Mr. Grumps a ticket. Don and Jon were glad. They ran into the house laughing and said, "Guess what! Mr. Grumps got a ticket for running into Officer Orville. Isn't that great?"

Grandpa looked sad. "Poor Mr. Grumps," he said.

"But it was his fault," said Don. "He is mean."

"But we should never be glad when someone else has problems," said Grandpa. "We shouldn't be happy at another's trouble, even if we don't like that person. Mr. Grumps may have problems we don't know about. We should love him and pray for him, even if he isn't nice to us."

"Well," Don said, "I guess then we had better pray for WeeWak, too."

Let's pray about this:
Dear God, thank you for loving everybody. Help us to be kind to people who aren't kind to us.
In Jesus' name, Amen.

No Vacation

It was Bible story time. Miss Pl
said, "Have you heard of Jonal
in the Bible who disobeyed Go
Lord gave him a special messa
'Preach to the city of Nineveh.'
Jonah hated Nineveh.

"Well," said Miss Plumper, 'sucn a
thing should be deplored, but foolish
Jonah just ignored the special message
from the Lord. He said, 'Some other

land should be explored, but not the
place picked by the Lord.' So Jonah
went on vacation. He found a trip he
could afford and paid the fare and went
on board. He yawned and dozed and
snoozed and snored until the mighty
tempest roared. The lightning flashed.
The rain downpoured. And Jonah
tumbled overboard."

"What happened then?" cried Don.

"He was swallowed by a great fish," said Miss Plumper. "And he didn't like it. It was smelly. He feared he would just turn into jelly inside that stinking fish's belly. So he told God he was sorry for disobeying. The Lord forgave him, and the fish hiccuped him out. Do you think Jonah went on to Nineveh? Do you think he learned to obey the Lord?"

And all the children said, "I should think so."

Let's talk about this:
Who disobeyed God? What happened to him?

Bethlehem . . . you are one of the smallest towns. —Micah 5:2
Read: Micah 5:2–4

Another Tiny Town

Lopez swung at the ball and missed. He dropped his bat and sat down in the dirt. "I know what is wrong with me," he said. "I'm too little."

"No, you are not," said Chipper, laughing.

But Lopez nodded his head up and down sadly. "Yes, I am, Chipper. I'm six, and Don and Jon are only five. But they are bigger than I am. There is something wrong with me," he said. "Why did God make me so little?"

Chipper put his hand on his friend's shoulder. He said. "You are not too little, pal. I was about your size when I was six. But hey, God makes us all differently. Some are big and some are small. And sometimes, small is good. Like Tiny Town. I like living here even though it's tiny, don't you?"

"Well, yes," said Lopez.

"Jesus was born in a small town. Bethlehem. But it was big in God's eyes.

Size isn't important at all. Small towns and small people can do big things when they want to. They can be big in God's eyes. Now grab that bat and stop feeling sorry for yourself."

Lopez jumped to his feet and grabbed his bat. He hit the ball. Hard. Not quite out of the park. But almost.

Let's pray about this:

Dear God, thank you for making us just the way we are. Help us to love all your gifts, whether big or little.

In Jesus' name, Amen.

The LORD is powerful, yet patient. —Nahum 1:3
Read: Nahum 1:1–3

Powerful but Patient

Angela threw the crayons across the room. Miss Plumper came over and sat down beside her. "Now look at this!" she said. "I'm afraid you have broken some of our crayons." Angela stuck her thumb in her mouth.

"Angela, why did you throw your crayons?"

"'Cause," said Angela.

"'Cause why?" asked Miss Plumper.

"'Cause I can't thtay in the lines."

Miss Plumper smiled. "It takes time to learn to color in the lines, Angela. You need to grow a little bit more. Soon you will be able to color in the lines." Angela took another suck on her thumb.

"Angela, the Lord is never in a hurry. He is very powerful, but very patient. He is helping you grow at just the right speed. Don't get upset with yourself. Give yourself time to learn. God is patient, so you should be, too."

Angela and Miss Plumper picked up the crayons, and they colored a picture together. Angela laughed when Miss Plumper got outside the lines once, too. "Don't get upthet, Mith Plumper," said Angela. "God ith patient, tho you thould be, too."

Let's talk about this:
Why did Angela throw her crayons? Is God patient?

Barker's Barks

Bark! Bark!"

"Bark! Bark! Barker Bark!" Everyone ran to the kitchen to see why Barker was barking.

"Oh, my goodness!" cried Mrs. Kisser. A pot holder on the stove had caught fire. Kim ran to the phone and called Firefighter Fritz. Her mother grabbed the fire extinguisher. Whish! By the time Firefighter Fritz arrived, the fire was out and everything was quiet.

"Barker saved us," Kim told Firefighter Fritz.

Later Mrs. Kisser sat on Kim's bed. "Barker really saved us," Kim said. "He saved us from a bad fire. Maybe he saved us from being hurt."

Her mother nodded. They were proud of Barker.

"And Kim," said Mrs. Kisser, "Jesus saves us in a different way. He died on the cross to save us. He saves us from being punished for doing bad things. God is able to forgive us because Jesus took our punishment. That is why we call him our best Friend. That is why we love him so much. That is why we trust him and ask him to forgive our sins."

Kim nodded again. She was proud of Jesus.

She fell asleep that night feeling very, very safe.

Let's pray about this:
Dear God, thank you for sending Jesus to save us from our sins. Help us to love him as we should.
In Jesus' name, Amen.

I Love You

Mrs. Martinez was tired. She had worked all day while Luis had been at Preschool Playhouse. Lopez had spent the day with Chipper, and he was tired, too. They were too tired to cook supper, so Mrs. Martinez said, "Let's go to Grab-a-Burger."

"No!" said Luis. "I don't want a Grab-a-Burger burger."

Mrs. Martinez felt angry. "Luis! I'm too tired to put up with this."

"No!" shouted Luis. "No! No! No!" He stomped his feet, and his mother left the room.

"Luis," said Lopez after a moment, "I don't want to go to Grab-a-Burger either, you know."

"You don't?" said Luis with a sniffle.

"No," said Lopez. "But Mommy is tired. She takes good care of us, and sometimes we need to take care of her. She's too tired to cook tonight."

Luis was sorry he shouted and stomped his feet. He and Lopez found their mother and hugged her. "We love one another very much," said Mrs. Martinez, her arms around the boys. "And Jesus loves us very much. His love helps us when we're tired or cross."

Luis smiled suddenly and his stomach growled. He felt hungry—hungry enough for a Grab-a-Burger burger with extra pickles.

Let's Talk About This:
How do you think Ms. Martinez felt when Luis shouted and stomped his feet? How did she feel when he hugged her?

Cheer up! Because I, the LORD All-Powerful, will be here to help you. —Haggai 2:4
Read: Haggai 2:3–9

Cheer Up!

What is wrong, Theo?" asked Mrs. Watts.

"Nothing," said Theo, looking sad.

"But you look like you have stepped on a nail again," she said.

Theo sighed. "Don and Jon can't come over to play," he said.

"What about Lopez or Luis?" asked Mrs. Watts.

"They are camping at the lake," said Theo.

"What about Chipper?"

"He is not home," said Theo. "And I'm bored."

"Why don't you ask the Lord for something interesting to do?" said his mother. "The Bible says, 'Cheer up! Because I, the LORD All-Powerful, will be here to help you.' The Lord can help you find something to do."

Theo went outside and walked around. He decided to do what his mother suggested. "God," he said, "I'm bored. Please help me find something to do." Just then he looked up and saw Firefighter Fritz washing the fire truck. He walked over. "Need some help?" he asked.

"Yep," said Firefighter Fritz. "I was just hoping someone would come along to help me." Theo grinned. He pulled off his shoes and got to work.

Let's pray about this:
Dear God, thank you for being all-powerful and for helping us in so many ways. Help us to stay busy for you.

In Jesus' name, Amen.

The Lord's Eyes

Jon, have you seen Don?" called Grandpa.

"No," shouted Jon. He didn't know that Don was under the little table near the sofa, hiding under the tablecloth. Grandpa looked in the backyard. He looked in the front yard. He looked across the street into the park. He said, "I'm getting worried. I think I will ask Officer Orville to look."

Don giggled so loudly that Grandpa lifted the tablecloth. "Don," said Grandpa, "I have spent half an hour looking for you. I was getting worried."

"I'm sorry," said Don. "I was just playing hide-and-seek. I found a place where no one could see me."

"Well," said Grandpa, smiling a bit, "you did find a good hiding place, but one person knew where you were."

"Who?" asked Don.

"The Lord Jesus. He always knows where we are. The Bible says, 'The eyes of the LORD . . . see everything on this earth.' He always knows where we are and what we are doing. He is always watching us. And you know what, Don? I'm glad."

"Me, too," said Don. "That means we can never get lost from him."

Let's talk about this:
Where was Don hiding? Who saw him there?

Bring the entire ten percent into the storehouse. —Malachi 3:10
Read: Malachi 3:8–12

Giving to God

What are you doing?" Kim asked her dad and mom. They were at the kitchen table with papers scattered around them.

"We are paying bills," said Mr. Kisser. "I got paid today, and I have put the check in the bank. Now we must write checks to other people."

"Like the gas company," said Mrs. Kisser, "and the water company. And we set some money aside for food and clothes."

"And most important," said Mr. Kisser, "we give money to the Lord. We write a check for Tiny Town Church."

"Here is your allowance, Kim," said her mother, handing her some money. "You should give some of your money to the Lord, too."

"I should?" asked Kim.

"Yes," said her father. "Jesus has given us all we own. He gives your mother and me strength and jobs to earn money. He provides for your allowance each week, too. So we should all give something back to the Lord. We should put something in the offering plate each Sunday."

The next Sunday, Kim gave the Lord Jesus some of her money. She smiled. She was happy. She was worshiping God.

Let's pray about this:
    Dear God, thank you for meeting all our needs.
    Help us to honor you with our money.
                        In Jesus' name, Amen.

Give us our food for today. —Matthew 6:11
Read: Matthew 6:7–13

I Like This Cake!

Miss Plumper had taken all the
preschoolers to Grab-a-Burger for lunch.
It was her birthday, and Officer Orville
brought a big birthday cake, dripping
with icing. There were 60 candles on it.

"Where did this cake come from?"
asked Miss Plumper, surprised.

The children had many answers: It
came from the kitchen; it came from the
cook; it came from the oven; it came
from a box. Theo said, "It came from
flour and sugar." He had seen his
mother make cakes.

Miss Plumper, nodding, said, "Cakes
are made from flour."

Angela said, "What kind of flowerth?
Hollyhockth?"

"Not flowers," said Miss Plumper
with a chuckle. "Flour. And where does
flour come from?" she asked.

No one knew. "From wheat," said
Miss Plumper. "And wheat comes from
seeds planted in the dirt. And it all
comes from God. He made seeds. He

made rain to water them. He made sunshine to grow them. And he gave us muscles to harvest them. Everything we eat comes from God. That is why we thank him for our food."

"That is why I like this cake!" said Luis.

Let's talk about this:
  How old is Miss Plumper? Where did her cake come from?

Water Walk

Jon and Don rubbed their eyes and raised up in their sleeping bags. Grandpa had built a little fire and was scrambling eggs. Their camping spot was right beside the lake, and it was a beautiful day.

Grandpa and Don and Jon thanked the Lord for their food. As they ate their breakfast, they watched a family of ducks swim across the lake.

"I wish I could swim across the lake," said Don.

"You will one day," said Grandpa. "You are a good swimmer."

90

"I wish I could just walk over the lake," said Jon.

"That is silly," said Don. "No one can do that unless the lake is frozen."

"One person can," said Grandpa. "Once when Jesus' friends were in a storm, they were frightened. They thought their boat was going to flip over in the waves. Jesus knew they were in trouble, so he walked across the water as though it were a sidewalk. He came walking on the water to help them. He made the storm die down."

"Wow!" said Don. "He must be very great."

"He is," said Grandpa. "And very caring. He cares about us and he is able to help us every day. That is why we love him so much."

Let's pray about this:
Dear God, thank you for the Lord Jesus. Help us to learn how powerful and loving he is.
In Jesus' name, Amen.

Everything he does is good! —Mark 7:37
Read: Mark 7:31–37

Hollyhocks

Knock! Knock! Knock! Knock!
Grandpa hurried to the door. It was Mr.
Grumps, and he looked unhappy. He
said, "Your two grandsons ran through
my hollyhocks. I worked all summer on
those flowers, and now your boys have
ruined them."

Grandpa was upset. "Don and Jon!"
he shouted.

But Don said, "We didn't do it,
Grandpa. We love hollyhocks."

Jon said, "I know who ran through
Mr. Grumps's flower bed. I saw Clyde
yesterday. He stepped on every flower.
He thought it was a game."

Mr. Grumps mumbled something and
went home.

"Mr. Grumps is a bad person," said
Jon. "And so is Clyde."

"Now, boys," Grandpa said, sitting
down on the front steps, "maybe Mr.
Grumps and Clyde upset us sometimes.
But not one of us has obeyed God all
the time. The Lord forgives us, and we

must forgive others. Only one person did nothing wrong. That was Jesus. He never sinned against God in any way. Everything he does is good." The boys nodded their heads.

"Now," said Grandpa. "Let's get our spades. We need to help Mr. Grumps with his hollyhocks."

Let's pray about this:
> Dear God, thank you for the Lord Jesus who is perfect in every way and without sin. Help us be more like him.
>
> In Jesus' name, Amen.

So That Is Who Jesus Is!

Kim Kisser had been reading her Bible in the gospel of Mark. She was curious about something. "Daddy," she said, "who was Jesus?"

Mr. Kisser put down his paper. He said, "Jesus is God's Son who came to die on the cross and save us from our sins."

Kim didn't understand that, so Mr. Kisser explained, "God made us. He made stars and planets and birds and bees and every person on earth. And he wanted us to be happy, so he gave us a special book telling us how to be happy. He gave us his rules in the Bible. But we have all disobeyed the Bible. And when we disobey the Lord, we aren't happy anymore. And God isn't happy with us, even though he still loves us. He knows that disobedience always needs to be punished."

Kim felt bad about that. But her father continued, "That is why Jesus came to planet earth. He let himself be nailed to a big wooden cross where he died to take our punishment. After he died, he was buried, but he came back to life three days later. He is alive right now, living in heaven, and he is able to watch us and love us and be with us all the time."

Kim thought about it for a moment. "So that is who Jesus is!" she said.

Let's talk about this:
    What did Kim want to know? What did Jesus do for us?

She dressed him in baby clothes and laid him on a bed of hay. —Luke 2:6
Read: Luke 2:5–12

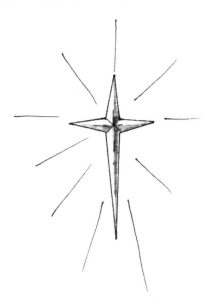

A Bed of Hay

All the children gathered around for Miss Plumper's Bible story. She said . . .

"Do you know who was born on Christmas Day? I will give you a hint. In a far-off land many years ago, on a starry night with the moon aglow, a lovely girl with her husband, Joe, found a vacant barn for their Baby-o.

"He was wrapped in cloth, nestled in the hay, and the shepherds came to call that day. The angels, too, would have their say. And wise men tramped from far away.

"The Babe was sweet, almost never cried. And Mary and Joe were so filled with pride that they smiled and cried as they sang and sighed, full of love and joy on that Christmastide.

"And the Baby grew, as all babies do. He learned to dress and to put on his shoes. He learned to teach what is wise and true. And he came to die for me and you."

"Now," said Miss Plumper, "who was this Babe asleep in the hay? This special Babe of Bethlehem?"

And all the children said, "I should say . . . Jesus!"

Let's talk about this:
Who was born on Christmas Day? Where did he sleep?

Prettier Than Tiny Town Lake

I wish WeeWak would die," said Don.

"Don," said Grandpa sharply, "we don't want anything to die."

"But he growls at me, Grandpa. Someday he is going to bite me."

"God made him and gave him life," said Grandpa. "I hope he lives a long, long time."

"What happens when something dies, Grandpa?" asked Don.

"Well," said Grandpa. "I don't know about animals, but I know about you and me. We go to be with Jesus in heaven. We will all be together there. Jesus wants us to be happy forever and ever, and he has a place for us much more beautiful than this world. We can look forward to it like a trip."

Don smiled. He liked trips. Grandpa continued, "When Jesus died, he didn't stay dead. He came to life again. All of us who know him will do the same. That is one reason we want to live for him now."

Don thought about it a moment. "Is heaven more beautiful than Tiny Town Lake?" he asked.

"Good heavens, yes!" said Grandpa. "Even prettier than Tiny Town Lake."

Let's pray about this:
Dear God, thank you for Jesus who died for us and came back to life. Please be our best Friend now and always.

In Jesus' name, Amen.

God loved the people of this world so much that he gave his only Son, so that everyone who has faith in him will have eternal life and never really die.
—John 3:16
Read: John 3:16–18

Chipper's Favorite Verse

"Chipper, what is your favorite Bible verse?" asked Lopez.

"Well, hey," said Chipper. "I like a bunch of them. There is one called 1 Thessalonians 5:16 that I like a lot. It says, 'Always be joyful.'"

"That is short," said Lopez.

"Well, hey, that is why I like it," said Chipper. "I memorized it really fast."

Lopez laughed. "But what is your very favorite verse, Chipper?"

Chipper thought about it a moment. "I guess it would be the most famous verse in the Bible," he said. "John 3:16. It says, 'God loved the people of this world so much that he gave his only Son, so that everyone who has faith in him will have eternal life and never really die.'"

"Wow, that is a long verse," said Lopez.

"Yeah," said Chipper. "But it's easy to learn. You could memorize it in no time.

It's important because it tells us why Jesus came to earth. God loved us even though we had disobeyed him. He sent his Son Jesus to die for us so that we can be forgiven. When we know Jesus, we have eternal life."

"Chipper," said Lopez. "Can I start with, 'always be joyful'?"

Let's talk about this:
    What is the most famous verse in the Bible? Do you think you could memorize it?.

Lakisha's New Book

Heeeelp!" cried Lakisha as she tried to open the front door. Her arms were too full of books, and they all tumbled onto the steps. As Lakisha picked them up, her mother came to the door.

"Where did you get all those books?" she asked.

"At the school library," said Lakisha. "I guess I got carried away."

"Well, I have another book for you," said her mother.

"Another one?" asked Lakisha as she followed her mom to the kitchen. Her mother handed her a beautiful new Bible, and on its leather cover was Lakisha's name in golden letters.

"The Bible is God's special book," said her mother. "It's different from all these other books. The Bible really has sixty-six smaller books inside it, and they all tell us about God's Son, Jesus."

Lakisha opened her new Bible. It was beautiful.

"You should read and memorize verses in the Bible every day," said her mother. And that night Lakisha didn't even get around to reading her armful of books from the school library. She was too busy reading her new Bible, the book that tells about Jesus.

Let's pray about this:
Dear God, thank you for the Bible. Help us to read and memorize and obey it every day.
In Jesus' name, Amen.

Coming Back

Angela, Abbie, and Chang watched
the sun drop lower in the sky. The clouds
piled up like giant marshmallows, and
the air seemed on fire. The sky swirled
with red and pink and white, all mixed
together like paints smeared on blue
paper.

Clyde came by. "What are you no-
good kids doing?" he asked. But he
walked on past them without waiting for
an answer. WeeWak came by. They
were very still and he trotted past them.
Lopez ran by, racing toward the sliding
board. Firefighter Fritz came by,
stopping to chat.

"The sky is so beautiful," said Abbie. "But no one seems to notice."

"Ah, it is beautiful," said Firefighter Fritz. "A beautiful sunrise or sunset always reminds me that Jesus is coming back to planet earth. Know why?"

They shook their heads.

"Well, when Jesus left the earth, he just disappeared through the clouds. He went back to heaven. The Bible says he is coming back the same way. One day—we aren't sure when—he is coming back through the clouds. It's going to be a wonderful day, and I think the sky and clouds will be lit up in beautiful colors, just to welcome him back."

Let's talk about this:
What did Firefighter Fritz think when he saw the beautiful sky? When is Jesus coming back to earth?

The Lord sent his angel to rescue me. —Acts 12:11
Read: Acts 12:1–12

Peter the Preacher

It was Bible story time. All the children gathered around, and Miss Plumper said, "I want to tell you what happened to a man in the Bible named Peter. The king threw Peter into jail for telling others about Jesus, but did he stay in jail? Well, here is what happened:

"Swam! Slam! Bonker! Bam! Peter the Preacher was in a jam. Peter the Preacher was in a jail, sweating and swooning in a sweltering cell. Smelling and dwelling and yelling and telling the folks about Jesus; telling them proudly, telling them loudly in that jambering, jangling, jumbling jail. But Peter the Preacher fell fast asleep as he prayed to the Lord his soul to keep. And when Peter the Preacher started to snore, who should come walking through the door but an angel sent on a special chore to get Peter the Preacher up off the floor and to free him as he had been before.

"So Peter the Preacher, all smelly and sore, rose up from that filthy prison floor and followed the angel right out the door. And he went to his friends all prayerful and pale, he went with an incredible tale to tell, that all was well—that all was swell—that he would no longer dwell in that jambering, jangling, jumbling jail."

Let's pray about this:
Dear God, thank you for the angels who watch over us. Please keep us safe and sound, day and night.

In Jesus' name, Amen.

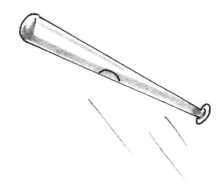

Me First!

Theo and Lopez wanted to play ball together, but they had a problem. They both wanted first bats. "You can't hit the ball," said Lopez. "Throw it to me and I will hit it. Chipper has been showing me how."

"No!" said Theo. "You throw first. I want to hit."

"No!" said Lopez. "You throw and I will bat first."

"No," said Theo. "Me first." He ran toward Lopez and rammed him in the stomach with his head. As Lopez fell, he grabbed Theo and pulled him down, too. Lopez jumped on top of Theo and held him down until he cried.

"Hey, what is going on here?" Both boys looked up when they heard Chipper's voice.

"He won't let me bat first, Chipper," said Lopez.

"Well, hey," said Chipper, "the Lord wants us to live at peace with each other. He doesn't want us to fight like this. I'm ashamed of both of you. Now, I want to see which of you gets to let the other bat first."

"I do!" said Lopez.

"No, I do!" said Theo.

Chipper laughed and laughed and laughed.

Let's talk about this:
    What were Lopez and Theo fighting about?
    What did Chipper want them to do about it?

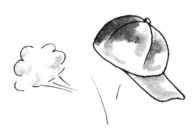

Love is kind and patient, never jealous. —1 Corinthians 13:4
Read: 1 Corinthians 13:1–5

Sad, Mad, or Glad

What is wrong, Lakisha?" asked Mrs. Watts. "You have looked mad all morning and sad all afternoon."

Lakisha folded her arms, stuck out her lip, and said, "I never get to go anywhere. Theo is going on a trip with Don and Jon. They are going to camp and swim and fish and even visit an amusement park. Why does Theo get to go and not me? I'm older than he is anyway."

Mrs. Watts said, "Let's talk about it over an orange soda." They went next door to Tiny Town Grocery, then walked to the park.

"Lakisha," said Mrs. Watts, "we are all going on vacation soon, but Don and Jon asked Theo to go with them on a little trip now because they are all the same age. They are all five years old, and they are buddies. Think of it this way. If you really love Theo, you will be glad he's getting to go with Don and Jon. Love isn't jealous. It wants good things to happen to other people. Love isn't selfish; it's kind and patient."

Lakisha thought about it a moment. She did love Theo. She loved him very much. So she decided not to be sad or mad any longer.

Just glad.

Let's pray about this:
Dear God, thank you for loving us and for helping us to love others. Please keep us from being jealous or selfish.

In Jesus' name, Amen

God loves people who love to give. —2 Corinthians 9:7
Read: 2 Corinthians 9:7–11

Thank You! Thank You!

It was snack time in Ms. Medina's classroom, and Kim Kisser pulled out three pieces of candy. She saw her friends pulling out their snacks, too. One boy had potato chips. Another had carrot sticks. And a nearby girl had a handful of homemade cookies. Kim ate her first piece of candy.

"Squawk! Excuse me! Excuse me!" said the parrot.

Kim noticed that Lopez didn't have a

snack. He must have forgotten his. He looked hungry. Kim popped her second piece of candy into her mouth.

"Squawk! Excuse me! Excuse me!" said the parrot.

Kim noticed Lopez looking at her last piece of candy. It was very good candy, and Kim wanted all three pieces. She was hungry, and the candy tasted so good. She started to unwrap it. She started to eat it.

"Squawk! Excuse me! Excuse me!" said the parrot.

"Excuse me," Kim said to Lopez, "but would you like a piece of candy?" Lopez took it and popped it into his mouth. He smiled.

Kim smiled. She knew that God loves people who love to give.

"Squawk! Thank you! Thank you!" said Excuse Me.

Let's talk about this:
Why didn't Kim want to give Lopez her candy?
How did she feel after she shared?

I Want to Race

"Lopez, will you play with me?" asked Luis. "I want to play racing."

"I don't feel like racing," said Lopez. Lopez didn't feel like playing with his little brother.

"Please, Lopez. I want to race."

Lopez was tired from school. But he knew his mother was tired, too. She had been at work all day. Lopez knew that she would cook them a wonderful supper anyway—maybe even pastrami pie, his favorite. He knew he should help her by playing with Luis.

"Come on, pal!" he shouted. "I will race you!"

The two boys raced from their house, past Mr. Grumps's house and on to Don and Jon's house. At the corner, Lopez helped Luis across the street, and they raced through the park. They ran and ran until Luis was too tired to run anymore. Then they swung on the swings and slid down the slides till they heard their mother calling.

She had made pastrami pie for supper.

Lopez was glad he had played with Luis. He didn't feel so tired now.

He had helped his mother.

Let's pray about this:
Dear God, thank you for helping us in many, many ways. May we never grow tired of helping others.

In Jesus' name, Amen.

The Greatest Thing

Bark! Bark! Barker Bark!" barked Barker. He tore off after a bird, but Kim didn't watch him. She was too busy sitting under a tree and thinking. Her father came near and sat beside her.

"I want to make sure Jesus is my best Friend," Kim told her dad. "I want to make sure I'm going to heaven one day."

Mr. Kisser said, "Well, the Bible says that we are saved by faith in God."

"Saved from what?" asked Kim.

"Saved from living without Jesus," said her dad. "Saved from punishment for our sins. We are saved by faith."

"What does that mean?" asked Kim.

"It means we believe that God loves us so much that he sent his Son to die on the cross for us. It means we believe it enough to ask God to forgive us for disobeying him. We trust Jesus to be our best friend and our Savior—the One who saves us. Kim," continued her dad, "we are saved by praying, by telling

God we are sorry for our sins and asking Jesus to be our Savior. That is the greatest thing in the world to do."

And that is exactly what Kim Kisser did.

Let's talk about this:
What was Kim Kisser thinking about? What did Kim Kisser do?

Do everything without grumbling or arguing. —Philippians 2:14
Read: Philippians 2:14–16

Mumbling and Grumbling

I don't want to pick up my crayons."

"I don't want to go outside."

"I don't want to stay inside."

"Luis won't share!"

Poor Miss Plumper. The Playhouse children had grumbled and argued all day. Finally she sat them all down and read them a poem. It said,

"What do you do with children who mumble?

With storms that rumble?

With feet that stumble, and cakes that crumble?

What do you do with fingers that fumble and bees that bumble?

With children who grumble and won't be humble?

Read them the Bible! Help them to see that only the Lord can humble

a rumbling, stumbling, crumbling,
fumbling, bumbling grumbler like you
and me."

"So," said Miss Plumper, "do
everything without grumbling or
arguing. Then you will be the pure and
innocent children of God.'"

And all the children took it to heart.

Let's pray about this:
Dear God, thank you for telling us to do everything without grumbling or arguing. Help us take it
to heart.

In Jesus' name, Amen.

Living in a Turkey

Chipper, can you play ball with me?"
Lopez shouted as loud as he could, but
Chipper couldn't hear him. The lawn
mower was too loud.

"Chipper!" Lopez yelled again,
jumping up and down on the sidewalk
and waving his arms. Chipper saw him
and turned off the mower.

"Hi, Lopez!" he said, coming nearer.

"Can you play ball with me,
Chipper?" asked Lopez.

"Not now. I'm mowing Mr. Grumps's
lawn."

"What are you mowing his lawn for,
Chipper?" asked Lopez.

"I need the money," said Chipper. "I

give ten dollars each month to a friend of mine in Turkey."

"He is in a turkey?" asked Lopez.

"No," Chipper said, laughing. "He is in the nation of Turkey. He is there to tell people about Jesus. He is a missionary. I mow lawns to help support him. You know, Lopez, the message of Jesus is spreading all over the earth. Maybe someday you will be a missionary."

"Would I have to live in a turkey?" asked Lopez. Chipper laughed and laughed as he headed back to his lawn mower.

Let's talk about this:
    Why was Chipper mowing Mr. Grumps's lawn?
    What is a missionary?

Children must always obey their parents. —Colossians 3:20
Read: Colossians 3:15–21

Don't Tease WeeWak

Boys, don't tease WeeWak," Grandpa said.

"Oh, we would never tease WeeWak," said Don and Jon. Grandpa strolled down to Grab-a-Burger to have coffee with Officer Orville. While he was gone, the twins played in the backyard.

"I have an idea," said Don. He ran to the kitchen and came back with an old pork chop. He pushed aside some leaves from the hedge and pushed the pork chop through. WeeWak saw it. He smelled it. He opened his mouth. Chomp! Don pulled the pork chop away just as WeeWak's teeth snapped together.

Jon laughed. "Let me try it," he said. He pushed the pork chop through the hedge and jerked it away just as WeeWak started to bite it. He tried it again, but WeeWak was too fast. His teeth clamped down on the pork chop. His teeth also clamped down on Jon's finger.

"Oww!" Jon shouted. He pulled his hand through the hedge, and WeeWak's teeth marks were in his finger. It was bleeding.

He had broken God's rules.

He had disobeyed his grandpa.

Let's pray about this:
Dear God, thank you for giving us rules. Help us to always be obedient.

In Jesus' name, Amen.

The Lord will return from heaven. —1 Thessalonians 4:16
Read: 1 Thessalonians 4:13–18

Homesick

I miss Daddy," said Kim Kisser. "When will he be back?"

"Not for two more weeks," said her mother. "He is away on business."

Kim felt homesick for her father. He had already been gone a week, and there were two more weeks to go.

"Why don't you get busy doing something useful?" said Mrs. Kisser. "It will help the time pass faster."

"Two whole weeks," said Kim.

Mrs. Kisser sat down beside Kim. "I miss him, too," she said. They were quiet for a moment, then Mrs. Kisser said, "I feel the same way about the Lord Jesus. I can't want for him to return."

"When will that be?" asked Kim.

"We don't know exactly," said Mrs. Kisser. "Jesus left the earth and disappeared in the clouds. But the Bible says he is coming back soon. The Bible says, 'The Lord will return from heaven.' I can't wait."

"Wow!" said Kim, thinking of both her dad and Jesus. "We sure do have a lot to look forward to."

"We sure do," said her mother. "We sure do."

Let's talk about this:
Where was Kim's father? Who else is coming back?

125

The Loafer

Clyde was sitting under a tree, feeling very lazy. He pulled a cigarette out of his pocket and watched Chipper mowing Mr. Grumps's lawn. He pulled a match from his other pocket. But when he struck the match, it broke. He got up and walked over to Chipper.

"Do you have a no-good match?" he asked.

Chipper stopped his lawn mower and looked at Clyde. "No," he said, "I don't smoke. Smoking is not good for you, Clyde. But I could use some help mowing this yard."

Clyde went back to his tree and sat down. He didn't feel like helping. Pretty soon Angela, Abbie, and Chang came running by. "Do you no-good kids have a match?" he asked.

"Of courth not," said Angela. "Why don't you run around the park with uth? Running ith good for you."

Clyde didn't feel like running. Pretty soon he heard Lopez call him. "Clyde, do you want to play ball?" Clyde didn't want to play ball. He was too lazy. He wanted to loaf.

Chipper, Angela, Abbie, Chang, and Lopez weren't loafers. They were workers.

Let's pray about this:
Dear God, thank you for giving us things to do. Help us to work hard for you. Keep us from being loafers.

In Jesus' name, Amen.

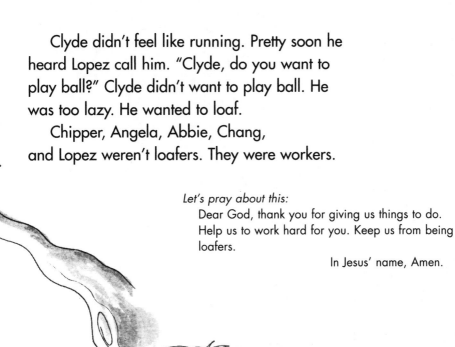

Glory will always be given to the only God, who lives forever and is the invisible and eternal King! —1 Timothy 1:17
Read: 1 Timothy 1:15–17

Why Theo Loves Storms

It was a big holiday in Tiny Town, and Firefighter Fritz had planned a fireworks display. He told everyone to go to Tiny Town Park at nine o'clock for a dazzling show of sparklers and boomers and sky bursts of color. But no one showed up. A thunderstorm blew in, and the rain poured in buckets. The thunder shook the houses.

Theo, very scared, crawled under the bed. But his dad came to find him. "Theo," said Mr. Watts, "didn't you want to see fireworks tonight?" Theo nodded his head. "Then come with me," said Mr. Watts.

128

Theo's dad lifted him into his arms and carried him to the front porch. Theo felt safe in his dad's strong arms. "These are God's fireworks," said Mr. Watts. Theo watched the jagged bolts of lightning tear through the sky. He could almost feel the thunder booming against his skin. He saw the rain pouring from the sky. It was something to see!

"God's fireworks are better than anyone's," said Mr. Watts. "He is the only God, who lives forever and is the invisible and eternal King. He sometimes sends storms to show us how wonderfully powerful he is."

And that was how Theo came to like thunderstorms.

Let's talk about this:
    Who had planned fireworks for Tiny Town?
    Whose fireworks did Theo watch?

129

Wise Lopez

Lopez watched his favorite program on television, but when it was over, he turned off the TV. He had not learned anything. His mind was not stronger. He picked up a comic book and read it cover to cover. Then he put it down and walked away. He had not learned anything. His mind was not happier.

He turned on the radio and listened to his favorite station. He heard a song he liked. Then he turned the radio off.

He had not learned anything very important, and his mind was not smarter.

He thumbed through the library book Ms. Medina had suggested. It was fun to read and interesting. He enjoyed reading a chapter of it, and his mind felt busy and active.

Then he picked up his Bible and read in 2 Timothy. He memorized a verse in chapter 3. As he read and memorized the Bible, he learned a lot. His mind felt fresh and strong. He felt closer to God. Now he knew why Chipper read the Bible so often. Lopez wanted to be like Chipper. And like Timothy, who since childhood had "known the Holy Scriptures," which made him "wise enough to have faith in Christ Jesus and be saved."

Let's pray about this:

Dear God, thank you for giving us eyes to read with, and a mind to learn. Please make us wise enough to have faith in Christ Jesus.

In Jesus' name, Amen.

Dogs, Cats, Snakes, and Worms

Angela, Abbie, and Chang were visiting Tiny Town Pet Store. They saw the puppy dogs, and Chang said, "Dogs are the best pets."

"That is because you have never had a cat," said Abbie. "My uncle Vesker has a cat named Snootykit that sits in my lap when I visit."

"I like thnaketh," Angela said.

"Snakes!" cried Chang. "Ugh! Gross! Slime!"

Abbie pushed over to the snake case and shivered. "There must be something wrong with you if you like snakes," she said.

Chang just said, "You are crazy, Angela. Dogs are the best pets."

"Cats!" said Abbie. The kids got into a loud fight.

"What a silly argument," said Officer Orville, hearing them. "Everyone likes different animals. No pet is best for everybody. Arguments like this are useless. God doesn't want us to argue. Anyway, as far as I'm concerned, the best pets are worms."

"Worms?"

"Yes," said Officer Orville. "They are easy to care for, they don't eat much—and they always go fishing with me."

Let's talk about this:
What were Abbie, Angela, and Chang fighting about? Is it usually wise to argue?

Oops!

Crash! Don and Jon looked at each other. They ran for Grandpa.

"We didn't mean to," said Don. "I hit the ball, and it went over the hedge and broke Mr. Grumps's window."

"Well," said Grandpa. "Maybe the Lord let it happen to give us a chance to tell Mr. Grumps about Jesus."

Grandpa, Don, and Jon went over to see Mr. Grumps. They told him they were sorry, and they replaced his window. Mr. Grumps smiled. He gave them all an orange soda, and they sat down to talk. Don and Jon didn't know Mr. Grumps liked orange sodas. They didn't know he smiled.

As they talked, Grandpa invited Mr. Grumps to church on Sunday. Grandpa told Mr. Grumps about Jesus.

Mr. Grumps listened.

Later, as Grandpa tucked Don and Jon into bed that night, he said, "Always look for a chance to tell others about Jesus." Grandpa turned off the light and turned to leave. He was almost out of the room when he thought of something else to say. "But," he said, looking right at Don and Jon, "that doesn't mean you can go around breaking any more windows!"

Let's pray about this:
Dear God, thank you for the Lord Jesus. Help us to tell others about him whenever we can.

In Jesus' name, Amen.

Some people have gotten out of the habit of meeting for worship, but we must not do that. —Hebrews 10:25
Read: Hebrews 10:21–25

Going to Church

Theo was in his climbing tree. He didn't have on shoes or shirt, and he felt very happy. "Theo," called his mother. "It's time to get ready for church." Theo didn't want to jump down. He didn't want to take a bath. He didn't want to put on nice clothes. He especially didn't want to put on shoes. He stayed in his climbing tree.

"Theo," called his mother. "Hurry!" Theo didn't move.

"Theo," called his mother again. "Come on!"

"I don't want to go to church," he said. "I like my climbing tree." His mother came out the door and into the backyard. She looked up at Theo.

"Who made your climbing tree?" she asked.

"God," said Theo.

"Who gave you hands and feet to climb with? Who gives you strength for climbing and playing? And who gives you beautiful days to enjoy?"

"God," said Theo.

"Well," said his mother, "don't you think you should go and thank him? I think you should worship him today."

Theo thought so, too. He jumped down and got ready for church.

Let's talk about this:
    Why didn't Theo want to go to church? Why did he decide to go anyway?

Be Glad

Kim Kisser looked under the pillows and crawled under the bed. She took every magazine from the rack and all the papers from the desk. She looked everywhere, but she couldn't find her library book.

"Ms. Medina will be angry," Kim told her mother. "I have lost my library book, and it's due tomorrow. I'm worried, and my stomach hurts."

Her mother said, "You shouldn't have been so careless, Kim. But I will help you. We will find it. And anyway, the Bible says to be glad, even when we have a lot of trouble."

"How can I be glad about losing a library book?" asked Kim.

"God can make bad things turn out good," said her mother. So Kim said a prayer and asked God to cause everything to turn out for good.

That night Kim went to bed without finding her book.

But the next morning, she looked underneath the car seat. And there it was—on top of the dollar bill she had lost the week before.

"God not only helped me find my book," she told her friends. "He used a lost book to show me where my dollar was. He can make even bad things turn out for good."

Let's pray about this:
    Dear God, thank you for blessing us with good things and for helping us through bad things. Help us be glad in all things.
                    In Jesus' name, Amen.

Bible Food

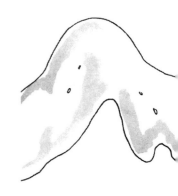

Kim Kisser entered the kitchen just as her dad tossed the pizza dough into the air. It whirled over their heads like a flying saucer and then fell—splat!—onto the floor. "Oops!" said Mr. Kisser. "Glad I have plenty of dough."

"Where is Mom?" asked Kim.

"Feeding Baby Kyle," said her dad, flattening another lump of dough.

"Baby Kyle sure eats a lot," said Kim.

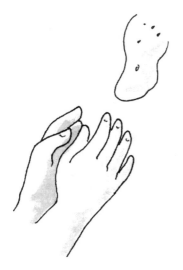

"Babies need lots of food," said her dad. "They are always hungry, and that is often why they cry. They are telling us they want some dinner. Food helps them grow. We all need food for our bodies. And we need food for our minds and hearts, too."

"We do?" asked Kim. "What kind of food?"

"Bible food," said her dad. "When

we read the Bible every day, we are feeding our hearts and minds. And that's just as important as eating supper."

Mr. Kisser tossed the dough into the air again. It whirled around like a flying saucer and landed—plop!—right in his hands.

"Think of it," he said with a smile, "as a meal for your mind. We should be as hungry as bears for God's Word."

"And as thirsty as newborn babies," said Kim.

Let's talk about this:
What was Mr. Kisser cooking for supper? What feeds our hearts and minds?

Best Best Friends

Chang and Abbie were going through the park. The wheelchair suddenly rolled over something, and someone cried, "Oww!"

"That is my toe," said Chipper, grabbing his sore foot. He had been sitting under a tree, reading his Bible. Abbie had not noticed where she was going.

"Sorry," said Abbie. "Chang and I were going for a walk."

"That is all right," said Chipper, still holding his toe and trying to smile. "But now we both need wheelchairs, Abbie." The kids laughed.

"Chang and I are best friends," said Abbie. "Along with Angela. We are the best friends in the world. Do you have a best friend, Chipper?"

"Well, hey," said Chipper, "I guess I have several. My girlfriend Georgette, of course. And Officer Orville and I are good buddies. And hey, I'm buds with the kids here in Tiny Town. But I have one best best friend."

"A best best friend?" asked Chang.

"Yeah," said Chipper. "The Lord Jesus. That is why I was reading my Bible before you ran over my big toe. I want to learn more and more about him. He is my best best Friend of all." Chipper picked his Bible up. "See you later, kids," he said. "Oh, and Abbie— watch where you are going."

Let's pray about this:
Dear God, thank you for being our best best friend. Please help us to keep learning more and more about you.

In Jesus' name, Amen.

If we confess our sins to God, he can always be trusted to forgive us. —1 John 1:9
Read: 1 John 1:6–9

'Fessing Up

Mr. Watts sat on the edge of Theo's bed. The lights were already off, and Theo felt sleepy. But something troubled him. "Daddy," he said, "I think God is mad at me."

"Why, Theo?" asked his dad.

"I threw a rock at WeeWak, and it hit him right on his bottom. He yelped. At first I thought it was funny. But Miss Plumper told us that God wants us to be kind. I think God is mad at me for throwing that rock."

"Well," said Mr. Watts, "it certainly makes God sad when we are mean to others. I'm sure He doesn't want you to throw rocks at WeeWak. But God forgives us when we ask him. You can tell God you are sorry for hitting WeeWak and ask him to forgive you."

So Theo closed his eyes and folded his hands.

"Dear God," he said, "I'm sorry I threw a rock at WeeWak, and I'm 'specially sorry it hit him. Please forgive me, and help me not to throw any more rocks at dogs. Not even at WeeWak. In Jesus' name. Amen."

Theo finished his prayer, but he didn't open his eyes. He was ready to go to sleep.

Let's talk about this:
Why did Theo feel bad? What did he do about it?

Since God loved us this much, we must love each other. —1 John 4:11
Read: 1 John 4:7–11

An Earful of Love

"**H**old hands while crossing the street,"
shouted Miss Plumper. Everyone looked
both ways. No car was coming, so they
walked quickly to the playground.
Angela jumped in a swing and started
pumping back and forth. Soon she was
flying high in the sky.

Luis walked by. He wasn't careful,
and he walked too near the swings.
Angela's foot hit him right in the ear.
Pow! Luis fell on the grass and cried.
Miss Plumper ran as fast as she could.
Angela jumped off the swing, and
Abbie came over to help, too. Miss
Plumper sat down on the grass and held

Luis in her arms. They looked at his ear, but it didn't seem badly hurt. So they all sat there a long time, helping Luis feel better.

"We love you, Luith," said Angela, sticking her thumb in her mouth.

Miss Plumper held Luis very tightly and said, "I should say so. We love you because the Lord Jesus gives us all love for one another. He loves us, and he helps us love one another. And that makes everything feel better—even hurt ears."

"I guess that is why I feel better already," sniffled Luis. He got up, wiped his nose—and beat Angela to the swing.

Let's pray about this:
    Dear God, thank you for loving us so much. Help us to love others just as you love us.
                        In Jesus' name, Amen.

Love means that we do what God tells us. —2 John 1:6
Read: 2 John 1:1–6

Real Love

Lopez, will you take these cookies to Firefighter Fritz?" Mrs. Martinez handed Lopez a bag full of freshly baked chocolate cookies.

"Can I do it later, Mom?" asked Lopez. He was watching his favorite TV show—Power Pals—and didn't want to miss any of it.

"No, he is waiting for them," said his mother.

"Can I finish my program first?"

"No, Lopez. Please take them now."

"Do I have to?" asked Lopez.

"Yes, Lopez. Now hurry."

So Lopez started down the street. He was sorry to miss his television show, but he wasn't mad about it. He would see it tomorrow. He was happy to help his mother. He loved her more than he loved the television. He loved her more than he loved his Power Pals on TV. He could watch his program anytime, but his mother needed his help today.

Lopez knew that love meant doing what his mother asked. He also knew that when he obeyed his mother, he was pleasing God. He was glad about that. His mom was glad. God was glad. And so was Firefighter Fritz.

Let's talk about this:
Why didn't Lopez want to take cookies to Firefighter Fritz? Why did he do it anyway?

Finders Keepers?

Don and Jon picked up the billfold and looked in it. It was full of cards and papers and money. Suddenly they heard someone approaching. "What are you no-good boys doing?" It was Clyde. "Where did you get that no-good billfold?" he asked.

"We just found it here," said Don. "Someone must have dropped it."

"You guys are lucky," said Clyde. "What are you going to do with it?"

"Give it to Officer Orville," said Don, "so he can find the owner."

"That is stupid," said Clyde. "You can buy a lot of no-good toys and games and stuff with all that money. Finders keepers. Losers weepers."

Don thought of the new baseball glove he wanted. Now he could buy it. Jon thought of orange sodas. Now he could buy all he wanted at Tiny Town Grocery. Both boys thought about Grandpa's birthday next week. Now they could buy him a nice present.

"Nope!" said Jon suddenly. "We are not going to let you talk us into stealing, Clyde. We are not going to copy you. We are going to take this billfold to Officer Orville right now."

And that is just what they did.

Let's pray about this:
Dear God, you want us to be more like Jesus.
Keep us from copying the evil deeds of others.
In Jesus' name, Amen.

Kept Safe

Thump! Crunch! Thump! Pitter-patter! Crunch! Crunch!

Kim Kisser lay perfectly still. The noises were over her head, in the attic. It sounded like someone crawling through the window and across the floor. She was too afraid to get out of her bed— and too afraid to stay in it.

So she slid one toe from under the covers and let it drop to the floor. She gave Barker a sudden jab with her

toenail. He woke up at once and started barking. Bark! Bark! Barker Bark! Barker Bark Bark Bark!

"Someone is upstairs," Kim said when her dad ran into the room. They quieted Barker and listened. Mr. Kisser smiled. "Kim," he said, "we have squirrels upstairs. I guess they have come over from Tiny Town Park and found a way into our attic. I will have to get them out tomorrow."

"They sure scared me," said Kim.

Her father said, "You know, Kim, you never need to be afraid at night. Your mother and I are in the next room. Barker sleeps here by your bed. And most of all, the Lord Jesus stays awake all night watching over you. The Bible says that we are kept safe by him." Mr. Kisser walked to the door. "Now," he said, smiling, "go back to sleep. And that goes double for you, Barker."

Let's talk about this:
   Why was Kim scared? Are you ever scared at

The Lamb who was killed is worthy to receive power. —Revelation 5:12
Read: Revelation 5:11–14

Can't Wait for Sunday!

I don't understand this verse," Lakisha told her dad. She pointed to a verse in her Bible. "It says, 'The Lamb who was killed is worthy to receive power.' Who is that talking about?"

Mr. Watts found his own Bible. He turned to the verse Lakisha was reading, Revelation 5:12. It was near the very end of the Bible.

"That is talking about Jesus," he said.

"Why did they call him a 'Lamb who was killed?'" asked Lakisha.

"Well, it's this way," said Mr. Watts. "Jesus is gentle like a lamb. But he died for us on the cross. Bad people killed him just as if he were a lamb. Jesus didn't stay dead, of course. He came to life again and walked out of his grave alive. Now the angels worship him. They want everyone to say that Jesus is powerful and wise and strong."

"That is what we do when we go to church, isn't it?" asked Lakisha.

"It sure is," said her dad. "When we go to church, we sing about Jesus."

"And talk about Jesus," said Lakisha.

"And pray in his name and study his Word," added Mr. Watts.

"Wow!" said Lakisha. "I can't wait for Sunday!"

Let's pray about this:
> Dear God, we want to worship you right now. Thank you that Jesus is worthy to receive power, riches, wisdom, glory, and praise.
>
> In Jesus' name, Amen.

Coming Again

Grandpa and Chipper had taken the twins camping. One night Grandpa asked them what they wanted for breakfast the next day. "Pancakes!" shouted Don and Jon.

"All right," said Grandpa. "I'll fix you pancakes over the campfire." But the next morning when the twins woke up, Grandpa was gone.

"Where is Grandpa?" asked Don. "And where are our pancakes?"

"Well," said Chipper, "your grandpa had a problem. He forgot the eggs, butter, syrup, flour, and milk. He has gone back to Tiny Town Grocery."

"He didn't have to do that," said Jon. "We could have had donuts."

"Well, hey," said Chipper, "your grandpa always tries to keeps his promises. If he promised pancakes, he will do it. Good people always try to keep their promises." Chipper watched the sun rise over the lake. "And Jesus always does," he said. "He has never,

ever broken one promise, and he never will. And his last promise is the best of all. He has promised to come back to earth. He said, 'I am coming soon!'"

"When do you think Jesus will come back to earth?" asked Don.

"Soon," said Chipper. "Real soon. Who knows—maybe today."

Let's talk about this:
    What has Jesus promised to do? When?

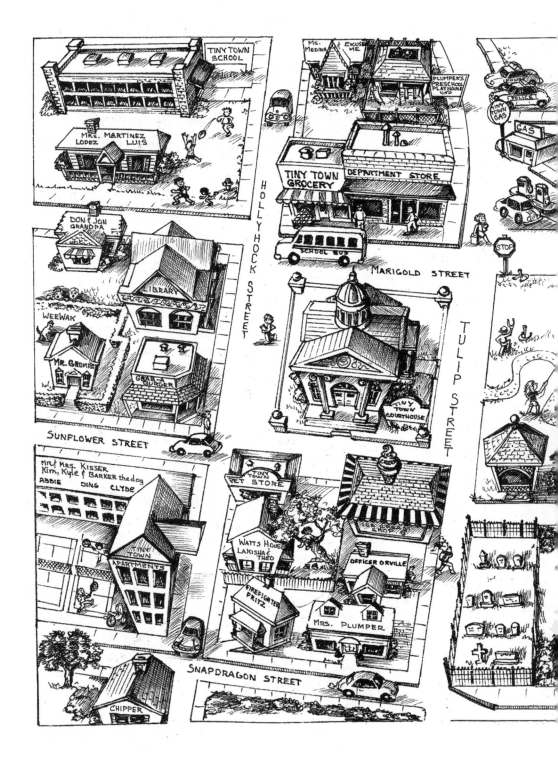

ROBERT J. MORGAN is a prolific writer whose articles have been published in several national evangelical magazines. He developed *Tiny Talks* to address parents' concerns about how to teach young children about the Bible. Since 1980, Morgan has pastored a suburban church in Nashville, Tennessee, where he lives with his wife, Katrina, and their three daughters.

ANN S. HOGUE, who is ranked among Missouri's top wildlife artists, teaches elementary art in Albany, Missouri, enjoys drawing children, and relates to the emotions and the likes and dislikes of the characters in Tiny Town. She and her husband, Gary, have two daughters and one son.